JOHN QUINCY ADAMS 1825–29	7 ANDREW JACKSON 1829–37	8 MARTIN VAN BUREN 1837–41	9 WILLIAM HENRY HARRISON 1841	JOHN TYLER 1841–45
ABRAHAM LINCOLN 1861–65	17 ANDREW JOHNSON 1865–69	18 ULYSSES S. GRANT 1869–77	19 RUTHERFORD B. HAYES 1877–81	20 JAMES A. GARFIELD 1881
WILLIAM HOWARD TAFT 1909–13	28 WOODROW WILSON 1913–21	29 WARREN G. HARDING 1921–23	30 CALVIN COOLIDGE 1923–29	31 HERBERT HOOVER 1929–33
RICHARD M. NIXON 1969–74	38 GERALD R. FORD 1974–77	39 JIMMY CARTER 1977–81	40 RONALD REAGAN 1981–89	41 GEORGE H. W. BUSH 1989–93

THE WHITE HOUSE HAS BEEN THE HOME
AND OFFICE TO EVERY PRESIDENT OF THE
UNITED STATES SINCE JOHN ADAMS.

Kids Play at the White House!

Illustrated by John Hutton • Text by Jonathan Pliska

THE WHITE HOUSE HISTORICAL ASSOCIATION

Introduction

Do you like to play outside? I think most kids do—even kids who live in the White House, the home of the president of the United States!

The president's children and grandchildren, as well as kids who are invited to attend special events like the Easter Egg Roll, have long known that the big backyard of the White House is a perfect place for children to play their favorite outdoor games. There are large open lawns with room for swing sets, paved pathways for bikes, big trees for tree houses, and space for make believe, organized sports, riding ponies, and playing with pets. Some of the White House kids' favorite activities might be your favorites too, like soccer and playing T-ball! Others may be new to you—like rolling a wooden hoop or riding in a cart drawn by a goat. Learning how kids have played in the White House backyard is a great way to learn more about the history of the White House, where the presidents have lived with their families for more than two-hundred years!

Let's Play!

Stewart D. McLaurin
President, White House Historical Association

The White House is the home and office
of the president of the United States . . . but many
of their kids have lived—*and played*—here too!
President Abraham Lincoln's son Tad liked to play
on the North Lawn dressed up like a soldier.

The soldiers guarding the White House were playmates for Tad Lincoln. He dressed up in his own matching uniform.

President Ulysses S. Grant's children
were often seen playing outside.
Nellie rolled a hoop and Jesse rode his bicycle.

A pet goat named "His Whiskers" often pulled President Benjamin Harrison's grandchildren around on a miniature cart.

Perhaps no one loved living in the White House more than President Theodore Roosevelt's six children. They had so many pets that the White House almost became a zoo. There were dogs, cats, guinea pigs, snakes, horses, toads, parrots, chickens, a badger, and even a bear!

President Franklin D. Roosevelt had a playground set up for his grandchildren in 1933, complete with a jungle gym, sandbox, and slide.

More than seventy-five years later, President Barack Obama's daughters Malia and Sasha played on a swing set in a spot nearby.

Caroline Kennedy liked to ride her pony, Macaroni, on the grass and even up to the windows of the Oval Office where her father President John F. Kennedy worked. John Jr. played nearby on the swing set.

President Dwight D. Eisenhower's grandchildren, David and Barbara Anne, rode their tricycles on the South Drive.

Amy Carter enjoyed climbing up
to the tree house personally designed
by her father, President Jimmy Carter.

President George H. W. Bush's many grandchildren played outdoor games. They especially liked to play with Millie's six puppies.

Even presidents without young children welcomed kids to play on the grounds. President George W. Bush hosted T-Ball games on the South Lawn.

President Bill Clinton's daughter
Chelsea played many sports growing up,
but soccer was one of her favorites.

President Donald Trump's son Baron also liked to play soccer. He had a goal set up in the East Garden.

From Lyndon B. Johnson to Joe Biden, presidential grandchildren have been putting their hand and footprints in the Children's Garden. Here kids watch the fish swim in the little pool and the furniture is kid-sized, just for them!

To
The White House Grounds
from
President and Mrs Lyndon B Johnson
Christmas 1968

Kids at play and outdoor fun are an important part of what make the White House a home.

About the Author

Jonathan Pliska is a landscape historian and author of *Presidents Play!* and *The White House Easter Egg Roll: A History for All Ages*. He lives in Baltimore County, Maryland.

About the Illustrator

John Hutton is a professor of art history at Salem College, where he has taught since 1990. He is the author of *How to Draw the Presidents* and has illustrated many children's books. He lives in Winston-Salem, North Carolina.

Chief Publishing Officer: Marcia Mallet Anderson; Senior Editorial and Production Director: Lauren McGwin; Senior Editorial and Production Manager: Kristen Hunter Mason; Editorial and Production Manager: Elyse Werling; Editorial Coordinator: Rebecca Durgin; Consulting Editor: Ann Hofstra Grogg

Original drawings by John Hutton are dedicated by the artist to Richard and Elaine Woodward, and to the memory of their son Stephen.
Copyright © 2022 by the White House Historical Association

10 9 8 7 6 5 4 3 2 1   Library of Congress Control Number: 2021953105   ISBN 978-1-950273-31-7   Printed in Italy

1 GEORGE WASHINGTON 1789–97	**2** JOHN ADAMS 1797–1801	**3** THOMAS JEFFERSON 1801–09	**4** JAMES MADISON 1809–17	**5** JAMES MONROE 1817–25
11 JAMES K. POLK 1845–49	**12** ZACHARY TAYLOR 1849–50	**13** MILLARD FILLMORE 1850–53	**14** FRANKLIN PIERCE 1853–57	**15** JAMES BUCHANAN 1857–61
21 CHESTER A. ARTHUR 1881–85	**22 & 24** GROVER CLEVELAND 1885–89, 1893–97	**23** BENJAMIN HARRISON 1889–93	**25** WILLIAM McKINLEY 1897–1901	**26** THEODORE ROOSEVELT 1901–09
32 FRANKLIN D. ROOSEVELT 1933–45	**33** HARRY S. TRUMAN 1945–53	**34** DWIGHT D. EISENHOWER 1953–61	**35** JOHN F. KENNEDY 1961–63	**36** LYNDON B. JOHNSON 1963–69
42 WILLIAM J. CLINTON 1993–2001	**43** GEORGE W. BUSH 2001–09	**44** BARACK OBAMA 2009–17	**45** DONALD J. TRUMP 2017–2021	**46** JOSEPH R. BIDEN 2021–